GRADE 5

The 2005–2007 Syllabus should requirements, especially those f sight-reading. Attention should Notices on the inside front cover, any changes.

The syllabus is obtainable from music retailers or from the Services Department, The Associated Board of the Royal Schools of Music, 24 Portland Place, London W1B 1LU, United Kingdom (please send a stamped addressed C5 (162mm × 229mm) envelope).

In exam centres outside the UK, information and syllabuses may be obtained from the Local Representative.

CONTENTS

Where appropriate, pieces in this volume have been checked with original source material and edited as necessary for instructional purposes. Any editorial additions to the texts are given in small print, within square brackets, or – in the case of slurs and ties – in the form ⌢. Fingering, phrasing, bowing, metronome marks and the editorial realization of ornaments (where given) are for guidance only; they are not comprehensive or obligatory.

DO NOT PHOTOCOPY © MUSIC

Alternative pieces for this grade

© 2004 by The Associated Board of the Royal Schools of Music

No part of this publication may be copied or reproduced in any form or by any means without the prior permission of the publisher.

Music origination by Andrew Jones.
Cover by Økvik Design.
Printed in England by Caligraving Ltd, Thetford, Norfolk.

A:1

Giga

Third movement from Sonata in D
'Les jeux olympiques', Op. 25 No. 5

Edited by
Hugo Ruf

CORRETTE

The French musician Michel Corrette (1707–95) was employed as a church organist throughout his long career, but he was also active as a teacher and composer. He wrote methods for many different instruments, including the violin, which provide useful information about 18th-century performance practice. The Op. 25 sonatas of 1742, from which this Giga is drawn (note the Italian title: a Frenchman here imitates a foreign style), are written for a combination that was becoming increasingly popular in the mid-18th century: 'for harpsi-chord with the accompaniment of a violin'. The title 'Les jeux olympiques' gives an idea of the rhythmic vitality needed to play this piece. The *forte* at the start has been added by the named editor. All other dynamics and all ornament realizations are suggested for exam purposes.

© B. Schott's Söhne, Mainz, 1968
Reproduced by permission. All enquiries for this piece apart from the exams should be addressed to Schott & Co. Ltd, 48 Great Marlborough Street, London W1F 7BB.

A:2

Con affetto

First movement from Sonata in A minor, Op. 5 No. 1

Edited by
Richard Jones

DEGLI ANTONI

Degli Antoni spent his life in Bologna, where, in addition to composing, he distinguished himself as a cornett player. Con affetto is a cantabile movement in the *grave*, classically restrained style that we associate with Corelli. The cadential figure ♩♪ is best phrased off thus: ♩♪
The many phrase repetitions invite echo dynamics. All dynamics, and all but the two-note slurs in bb. 1, 3, 5–6, 8, 10–11, 13 (first slur), 19 and 25, are editorial.

Source: *Suonate a violino solo col basso continuo per l'organo*, Op. 5 (Bologna, 1686)

Reproduced from *Baroque Violin Pieces*, Book 3, edited by Richard Jones (Associated Board)

Menuetto and Trio

Third movement from Sonata in G minor, Op. 137 No. 3, D. 408

A:3

Edited by
Richard Jones

SCHUBERT

Menuetto

Allegro vivace [♩ = *c.* 138]

[Last time only]

Fine

Trio

p dolce

Menuetto D.C.

In his late teens and early twenties Schubert was strongly influenced by the music of his compatriot Mozart. During this period – in 1816, when only 19 years old – he wrote three short violin sonatas which were not published until after his death, but have since become some of his most popular chamber works. The Menuetto and Trio are drawn from Sonata No. 3 in G minor. In the exam the da capo should be played, but none of the internal repeats. The slurs in bb. 21–8 of the violin part are editorial suggestions only. The staccato dots in bb. 49 and 61 of the violin part and in b. 61 of the keyboard part are in the source; all others are editorial.

Source: *Drei Sonatinen für Piano-Forte und Violine*, Op. 137 (Vienna: A. Diabelli & Co., 1836)

B:1

Album Leaf

No. 7 from *Lyric Pieces*, Op. 12

Arranged by
Josef Gingold

GRIEG

Edvard Grieg (1843–1907) wrote 10 sets of *Lyric Pieces* – miniature mood-pictures – which have long been favourites with pianists. Op. 12 is the first set, and was published in 1867.

AB 3005

B:2

Czardas

No. 3 from *Hungarian Sketches*, Op. 23

Edited by
Richard Jones

HILLE

Born in 1850 in Jerichow, near Berlin, Gustav Hille became a pupil of the great violinist Joseph Joachim. He emigrated to America and taught from 1880 in Philadelphia, directing his own conservatory there from 1910. *Czardas* aims to recreate the fire and passion of traditional Hungarian folk-dance music.

Source: *Bilder von der Puszta: Hungarian Sketches*, Op. 23 (London: Laudy & Co., 1906)

Berceuse

B:3

IRELAND

A *berceuse* (from the French word *berceau*, meaning 'cradle' or 'crib') is a gentle song designed for lulling children to sleep.

Jorvik

No. 2 from *Four York Pieces*

EDWARD HUWS JONES

Jorvik is the Viking name for York, which at the time was a thriving settlement and port, trading with Scandinavia. The opening music evokes the 'ings' – marshlands and water meadows of the River Ouse – with wide skies and the flight of birds. This leads to an energetic section prompted by the sounds of a Viking shipyard and the rhythm of the carpenters' axes. EHJ

C:2

The Silver Tears of the Moon

MICHAEL RADANOVICS

Originally from Brazil, the bossa nova is a musical style created from the samba and 'cool' jazz, as exemplified by the song *The Girl from Ipanema*.

Air and Pizzicato

SUGÁR

Air

Born in Budapest in 1919, Rezső Sugár was heavily influenced by Hungarian history and folklore.

Reproduced from *Violin Music for Beginners 2* by permission. All enquiries for this piece apart from the exams should be addressed to Editio Musica Budapest, Floor 5, Victor Hugó u. 11–15, H–1132 Budapest, Hungary.

Pizzicato

Checklist of Scales and Arpeggios

Candidates and teachers may find this checklist useful in learning the requirements of the grade. Full details of the forms of the various requirements, including details of rhythms, starting notes and bowing patterns, are given in the syllabus and in the scale books published by the Board.

Grade 5

			separate bows					slurred					
Major Scales								*two beats to a bow*					
	A♭ Major	2 Octaves											
	B Major	2 Octaves											
	C Major	2 Octaves											
	E♭ Major	2 Octaves											
	E Major	2 Octaves											
	G Major	3 Octaves											
Minor Scales (*melodic* or *harmonic*)								*two beats to a bow*					
	G♯ Minor	2 Octaves											
	B Minor	2 Octaves											
	C Minor	2 Octaves											
	E Minor	2 Octaves											
	G Minor	3 Octaves											
Chromatic Scales								*four* or *six notes to a bow*					
	on G	2 Octaves											
	on A	2 Octaves											
	on B♭	2 Octaves											
Major Arpeggios								*six notes (two-octave arpeggios) and three notes (three-octave arpeggios) to a bow*					
	A♭ Major	2 Octaves											
	B Major	2 Octaves											
	C Major	2 Octaves											
	E♭ Major	2 Octaves											
	E Major	2 Octaves											
	G Major	3 Octaves											
Minor Arpeggios								*six notes (two-octave arpeggios) and three notes (three-octave arpeggios) to a bow*					
	G♯ Minor	2 Octaves											
	B Minor	2 Octaves											
	C Minor	2 Octaves											
	E Minor	2 Octaves											
	G Minor	3 Octaves											
Dominant Sevenths								*four notes to a bow*					
	in B♭	1 Octave											
	in C	2 Octaves											
	in D	2 Octaves											
Diminished Sevenths								*four notes to a bow*					
	on G	1 Octave											
	on D	1 Octave											
	on A	1 Octave											

GRADE
5

RICHMOND *music* TRUST

The 2005–2007 Syllabus should be read for details of requirements, especially those for scales, aural tests and sight-reading. Attention should be paid to the Special Notices on the inside front cover, where warning is given of any changes.

The syllabus is obtainable from music retailers or from ￼he Services Department, The Associated Board of the Royal ￼chools of Music, 24 Portland Place, London W1B 1LU, ￼nited Kingdom (please send a stamped addressed C5 ￼62mm × 229mm) envelope).

￼ exam centres outside the UK, information and syllabuses ￼may be obtained from the Local Representative.

REQUIREMENTS

SCALES AND ARPEGGIOS (from memory)
in A♭, B, C, E♭, E majors; G♯, B, C, E minors (two octaves)
G major; G minor (three octaves)

Scales
in the above keys (minors in melodic *or* harmonic form at candidate's choice):
(i)   separate bows
(ii) slurred, two beats to a bow

Chromatic Scales
starting on G, A and B♭ (two octaves):
(i)   separate bows, even notes
(ii) slurred, four *or* six notes to a bow at candidate's choice

Arpeggios
the common chords of the above keys:
(i)   separate bows, even notes
(ii) slurred, six notes to a bow (two-octave arpeggios) and three notes to a bow (three-octave arpeggios)

Dominant Sevenths
in the keys of B♭ (starting on F and resolving on the tonic) (one octave) and C and D (starting on G and A and resolving on the tonic) (two octaves):
(i)   separate bows, even notes
(ii) slurred, four notes to a bow

Diminished Sevenths
starting on open strings G, D and A (one octave):
(i)   separate bows, even notes
(ii) slurred, four notes to a bow

PLAYING AT SIGHT (see current syllabus)

AURAL TESTS (see current syllabus)

THREE PIECES   *page*

Candidates must prepare three pieces, one from each of the three Lists, A, B and C. Candidates may choose from the pieces printed in this volume or any other piece listed for the grade. A full list is given in the current syllabus.

DO NOT PHOTOCOPY © MUSIC

Where appropriate, pieces in this volume have been checked with original source material and edited as necessary for instructional purposes. Any editorial additions to the texts are given in small print, within square brackets, or – in the case of slurs and ties – in the form ⌒. Fingering, phrasing, bowing, metronome marks and the editorial realization of ornaments (where given) are for guidance only; they are not comprehensive or obligatory.

A:1

Giga

Third movement from Sonata in D
'Les jeux olympiques', Op. 25 No. 5

Edited by
Hugo Ruf

CORRETTE

The French musician Michel Corrette (1707–95) was employed as a church organist throughout his long career, but he was also active as a teacher and composer. He wrote methods for many different instruments, including the violin, which provide useful information about 18th-century performance practice. The Op. 25 sonatas of 1742, from which this Giga is drawn (note the Italian title: a Frenchman here imitates a foreign style), are written for a combination that was becoming increasingly popular in the mid-18th century: 'for harpsichord with the accompaniment of a violin'. The title 'Les jeux olympiques' gives an idea of the rhythmic vitality needed to play this piece. The *forte* at the start has been added by the named editor. All other dynamics and all ornament realizations are suggested for exam purposes.

4

A:2

Con affetto

First movement from Sonata in A minor, Op. 5 No. 1

Edited by
Richard Jones

DEGLI ANTONI

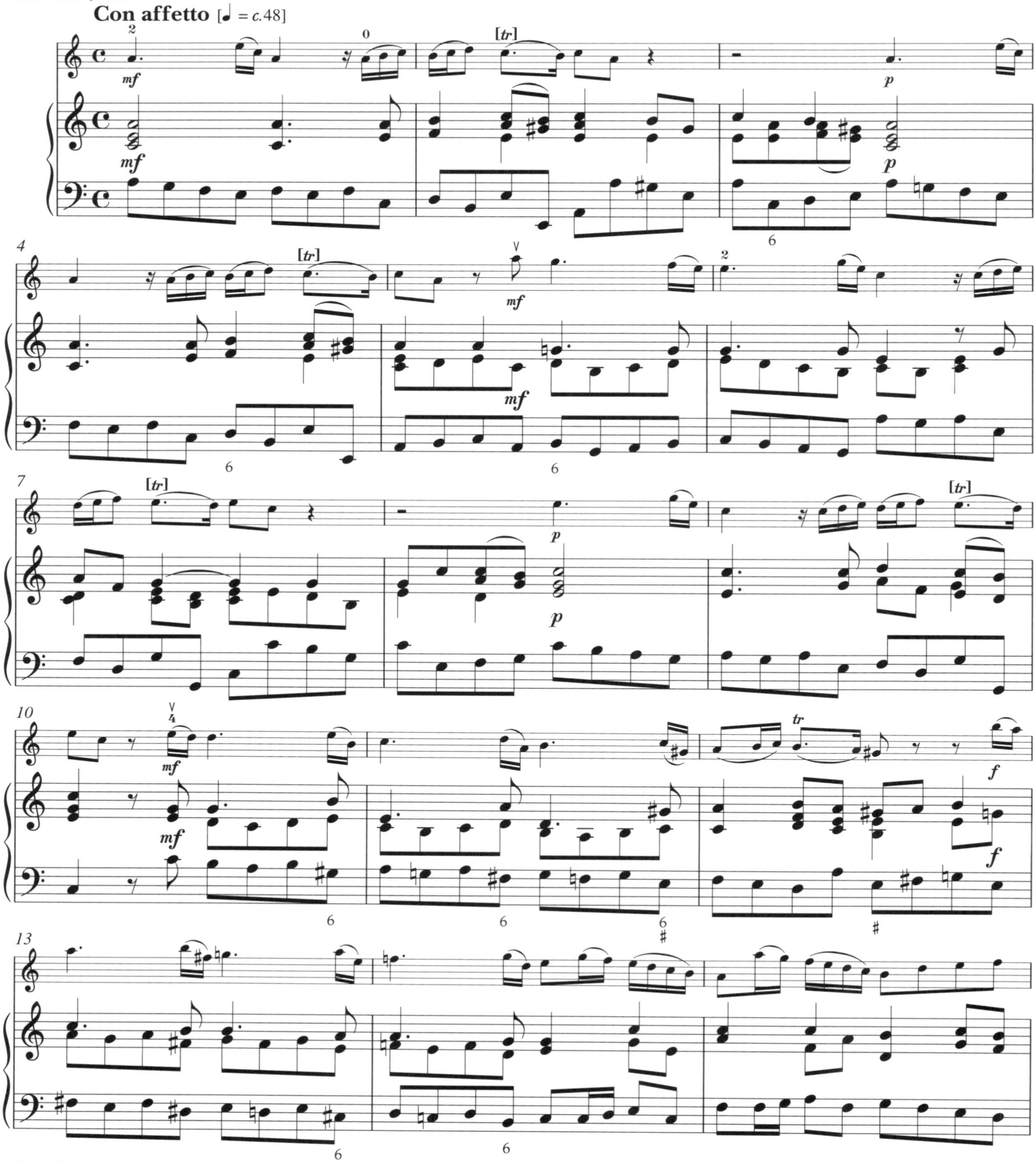

Degli Antoni spent his life in Bologna, where, in addition to composing, he distinguished himself as a cornett player. Con affetto is a cantabile movement in the *grave*, classically restrained style that we associate with Corelli. The cadential figure is best phrased off thus: The many phrase repetitions invite echo dynamics. All dynamics, and all but the two-note slurs in bb. 1, 3, 5–6, 8, 10–11, 13 (first slur), 19 and 25, are editorial.
Source: *Suonate a violino solo col basso continuo per l'organo*, Op. 5 (Bologna, 1686)

Reproduced from *Baroque Violin Pieces*, Book 3, edited by Richard Jones (Associated Board)

A:3

Menuetto and Trio

Third movement from Sonata in G minor, Op. 137 No. 3, D. 408

Edited by
Richard Jones

SCHUBERT

Menuetto

Allegro vivace [♩ = c.138]

In his late teens and early twenties Schubert was strongly influenced by the music of his compatriot Mozart. During this period – in 1816, when only 19 years old – he wrote three short violin sonatas which were not published until after his death, but have since become some of his most popular chamber works. The Menuetto and Trio are drawn from Sonata No. 3 in G minor. In the exam the da capo should be played, but none of the internal repeats. The slurs in bb. 21–8 of the violin part are editorial suggestions only. The staccato dots in bb. 49 and 61 of the violin part and in b. 61 of the keyboard part are in the source; all others are editorial.

Source: *Drei Sonatinen für Piano-Forte und Violine*, Op. 137 (Vienna: A. Diabelli & Co., 1836)

B:1

Album Leaf

No. 7 from *Lyric Pieces*, Op. 12

Arranged by
Josef Gingold

GRIEG

Edvard Grieg (1843–1907) wrote 10 sets of *Lyric Pieces* – miniature mood-pictures – which have long been favourites with pianists. Op. 12 is the first set, and was published in 1867.

AB 3005

B:2

Czardas
No. 3 from *Hungarian Sketches*, Op. 23

Edited by
Richard Jones

HILLE

Born in 1850 in Jerichow, near Berlin, Gustav Hille became a pupil of the great violinist Joseph Joachim. He emigrated to America and taught from 1880 in Philadelphia, directing his own conservatory there from 1910. *Czardas* aims to recreate the fire and passion of traditional Hungarian folk-dance music. In the piano part, the last LH note in b. 105 has been changed from D♮ to E by analogy with b. 9.
Source: *Bilder von der Puszta: Hungarian Sketches*, Op. 23 (London: Laudy & Co., 1906)

molto rit.   a tempo

Berceuse

IRELAND

B:3

A *berceuse* (from the French word *berceau*, meaning 'cradle' or 'crib') is a gentle song designed for lulling children to sleep.

Jorvik

No. 2 from *Four York Pieces*

EDWARD HUWS JONES

Jorvik is the Viking name for York, which at the time was a thriving settlement and port, trading with Scandinavia. The opening music evokes the 'ings' – marshlands and water meadows of the River Ouse – with wide skies and the flight of birds. This leads to an energetic section prompted by the sounds of a Viking shipyard and the rhythm of the carpenters' axes. EHJ

C:2

The Silver Tears of the Moon

MICHAEL RADANOVICS

Originally from Brazil, the bossa nova is a musical style created from the samba and 'cool' jazz, as exemplified by the song *The Girl from Ipanema*.

Air and Pizzicato

SUGÁR

Born in Budapest in 1919, Rezső Sugár was heavily influenced by Hungarian history and folklore.

Pizzicato

Allegretto [♩ = c.120]